# Apple Watch
# Series 5

## User's Guide

The Complete Beginners Guide to Mastering Your
iWatch Series 5

**Thomas Jackson**

# Copyright

# Table of Contents

Copyright ........................................................ iii

Why This Guide ................................................ x

About the Author ............................................. xi

Introduction ................................................... 1

What's in the box ............................................. 2

Setting up the charger ..................................... 4

To charge the Apple watch ............................... 4

Setting Up Your Apple Watch for The First Time ....... 6

Turn your Apple watch device on or off ................. 6

Connecting the device to your iPhone ................... 7

How to manually pair Apple Watch with iPhone .. 8

Signing in to your Apple ID ............................... 9

Setting up the passcode for your Apple watch ...... 10

Customization and Notifications .......................... 12

Renaming your Apple watch ...................................12

Customizing activity notification ...........................13

Customizing the mail notification ...........................17

To customize your mail notification ......................17

Customizing the message notification ....................18

To customize your message notification .................18

How to create custom message replies on your
Apple watch..................................................................19

To delete or change custom replies on your Apple
watch..............................................................................21

To prioritize or rearrange your message responses
........................................................................................21

Customizing the phone notification.......................22

What to do when custom notification is not
responding. ...............................................................22

Customization with Apple Watch Faces ................24

Changing watch faces on Apple watch ....................26

Adding Apple watch face to your list ..................... 27

Organizing the list of Apple watch faces ............... 28

Setting a photo as the Apple watch face ................ 29

How to delete an Apple watch face ......................... 31

Track Health and Fitness ............................................. 33

How to set up Activity on your Apple Watch ....... 33

Phone Calls on the Apple Watch ................................ 34

Answering Phone Calls with the Apple watch ...... 34

Apple Watch New Features .......................................... 35

How to turn Fall Detection on ................................... 35

How to Enable Wrist Detection ................................. 36

How to make an emergency call after a fall ........... 37

How to add friends and family to your emergency

contact list ................................................................... 38

Noise App ................................................................... 39

How to customize noise alerts ................................. 40

Hide Sensitive Information on the Watch Face ..40

Making Proficient Use of The Digital Crown ............42

Wake up your watch ................................................43

Home button........................................................43

App switch ...........................................................44

Zooming ..............................................................44

Restarting your watch ...........................................45

Scroll vertical Screens ...........................................45

Volume control......................................................46

Siri.......................................................................46

Take a screenshot ..................................................46

Quit an app ..........................................................47

Turn off display......................................................47

Time setting...........................................................47

Using digital touch to send sketches, heartbeat and
taps on the Apple watch ........................................48

Amazing Apple Watch Tips and Tricks...................... 50

Get Apple Watch to tell time ............................... 50

Locate your iPhone ............................................. 50

Mute alerts......................................................... 51

Enlarge on-screen text ........................................ 52

Take a screenshot ............................................... 52

Force restart....................................................... 52

Pre-compose messages ........................................ 53

Call holding....................................................... 53

Add and play music............................................ 53

Unlock your Mac................................................ 54

Take photos........................................................ 55

Use Siri on your Apple watch ............................. 55

Use pictures as watch faces................................. 56

Monitor data usage ............................................ 56

Water eject feature.............................................. 56

Enable the Mickey and Minnie feature ...............57

Clear notifications ....................................58

Mark mail messages ...............................58

Monitor activities ....................................59

Final Note ..........................................................60

# Why This Guide

So, you just got your Apple Watch, that's great! Now that you are here, we have detailed instructions you need to guide you through setting it up for the first time.

The Guides in this book are essentials for novice users who wish to the Apple Watch Series 5 with ease.

# About the Author

Thomas Jackson is a tech enthusiast with about 10 years' experience in the ICT industry. He is passionate about the latest technical and technological trends. Thomas holds a Bachelor and a Master's Degree in Computer Science and Information Communication Technology respectively from MIT, Boston Massachusetts.

# Introduction

So, you just got your Apple watch, that's great! Now that you are here, we have detailed instructions you need to guide you through setting it up for the first time. The Apple watch is a popular gadget that serves the function of a traditional watch, health and fitness tracker, timer and communication needs. It looks as perfect on a 10 years old kid as on a 70 years old adult, no age restriction.

With each watch series Apple rolls out, comes a better and user-friendly feature which has made it become an essential part of people's lives. Now that you have your new Apple watch, let's help you set it up and tailor it to your preference.

# What's in the box

In the newly bought package, you find two boxes; one which contains the watch and a slimmer box containing the watch straps or band.

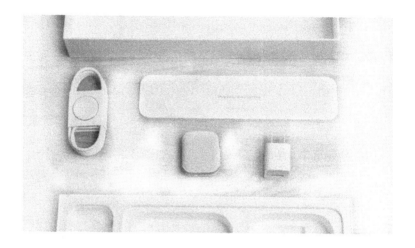

- USB wall adapter
- USB connecting cord (1m long)
- Watch body wrapped in a felt cover
- Watch band
- Instruction manual

Each of the items in the boxes has its own function. While the straps are to be fixed on the watch body, the charger is meant to keep the device charged. As with every new electronic device, the first step you take with your new device is to have it charged for some hours. It is not advisable to use your new Apple device without charging.

## Setting up the charger

Gently remove the Apple watch magnetic charging cable or dock and place on a flat surface. Plug it into a power adapter and then to a power outlet.

## To charge the Apple watch

Place your Apple watch magnetic charging cable on the back of the watch. The concave end of the charging cable will magnetically attach to the back of the watch until it is properly connected.

Once charging begins, you hear a beep sound and a charging indicator to show the charging progress. The indicator light is red when power is drained and green when charging is in progress or when fully charged. If your Apple watch comes with a magnetic charging dock, you can place your Apple watch in the dock or otherwise leave the watch to charge on its side or in a flat position with its bands open.

Your Apple watch automatically enters into the battery reserve mode once it the battery level drops to 10% with a beep or chime alert. When charged, you can return to normal power mode by restarting your device. To restart your Apple watch, you need to press and hold the side button until the Apple logo appears.

To monitor your Apple watch battery level and usage, you can add the battery complication icon on your device watch face. This will show you the battery percentage while in use. Once it is fully charged, your Apple watch is ready for use. Further in this guide, we'll show you the various steps to set up your new Apple watch.

## Setting Up Your Apple Watch for The First Time

With a fully charged Apple watch, you can now begin the setup process to get your watch working.

### Turn your Apple watch device on or off

To turn on your Apple watch for the first time, press and hold the side button until you see the Apple logo appear on the screen. It can be a blank screen at first but it is usually for a short time. Once it successfully comes on, a default watch face appears on the screen.

To turn off your Apple watch (which rarely occurs), hold down the side button as with when you turn on the device, but this time, until three sliders appear on the screen. Drag the power off slider to the right. You can only turn off your Apple watch when it's not charging. If charging, disconnect from its charger first before you switch off the device.

**Connecting the device to your iPhone**

The Apple watch cannot function without the iPhone, before you can start using your Apple watch, you need to first pair it with an iPhone. It should be noted that you must have an iPhone 5 or later in order to pair with an Apple Watch. You'll also need to make sure that the iPhone is running iOS 8.2 or later.

After you turn on your new Apple watch, pairing with your iPhone is usually the next step. You will need the Apple watch app or set up assistant pre-installed on your iPhone or from the app store.

Then wear your Apple watch on your wrist or bring it close to your iPhone until the Apple watch pairing screen appears on your iPhone then press '**Continue.**' Or rather open the Apple watch app on your phone and tap '**pair new watch**'.

At the prompt, place your Apple watch such that it appears on the view finder in the Apple watch app, this automatically pairs the two devices. To do this easily, ensure that you wear your Apple watch and hold it up to the camera and wait for a message to say your watch has been successfully paired.

Once paired, tap set up Apple watch and follow the instructions on your iPhone to finish setup. If the camera doesn't start the pairing process, you can tap the '**pair Apple watch manually**' icon at the bottom of your iPhone screen.

**How to manually pair Apple Watch with iPhone**

- Go to the Watch app on your iPhone.
- Click on 'Start Pairing'.
- Click on Pair Apple Watch Manually
- Tap 'I' on your Apple Watch to view the device's name.
- Then on your iPhone, select your Apple Watch from the list.

- Select if you are setting up the Apple watch from scratch or from a backup.

**Signing in to your Apple ID**

Once you are paired to your iPhone, the next is to sign into your Apple iOS account. Usually, your Apple watch will automatically sign into the Apple account of the iPhone you are connected to at the time of pairing. So, if asked, you can enter your Apple id password or better still sign in manually on your Apple watch app. Click general, then Apple id and then sign in.

If you can't sign in to your Apple id on your Apple watch, then one of these three is likely the cause

- Your Apple watch has been previously owned by someone
- Your Apple watch has been paired to another iPhone

- You need to update your Apple watch to the latest version of watchOS or be sure that the iPhone is working on the latest version of iOS

If your Apple watch has been previously owned by someone, you can contact the previous owner to remove its activation lock before you can continue set up. In cases when you forget your passcode, it is recommended that you erase your Apple watch and begin the setup again. If your Apple watch has been previously paired to another iPhone, you may need to un-pair from the former device and re-pair with the new device.

**Setting up the passcode for your Apple watch**

A pass code is usually not necessary for your Apple watch but may be needed for certain features like Apple pay. To set up a passcode, tap create passcode on your iPhone and do same on your paired Apple watch. To skip this process, you can easily tap don't add passcode.

## Customization and Notifications

Now that you are all set up, there are few changes you may like to make on your device to make it more personalized from its default settings. Let's walk you through the steps as you go on to customize your Apple watch.

### Renaming your Apple watch

As with other Apple devices, your Apple watch will be a new companion to keep tracks of your daily activities, therefore it deserves a name of its own right? Whatever name you decide for your Apple watch, here's how to go about it.

On your watch paired iPhone, open the watch app.

> ➤ Tap on the general icon

- ➤ Tap the about
- ➤ Tap on name
- ➤ Type your preferred name

There's no next, you just renamed your Apple watch.

Simplified, Open the watch app on your iPhone, tap general >about>name>type name> all done.

## Customizing activity notification

If you think your Apple watch is only to check time and send messages, you are in for loads of surprises. One of the many features you can enjoy whilst using your new Apple watch is its sync ability. This enables you to use your iPhone less especially when in the middle of a big task, on the run or somewhere your phone could pose a big distraction. You are able to view your apps notification and updates on your Apple watch without a glance on your iPhone. You can sync the notification actions to function similarly on both devices, that is, your iPhone and Apple watch and customize these notifications so you don't get distracted by unnecessary notifications.

How to customize notifications for Apple built-in apps on your Apple watch

➢ Go to Apple watch app on your iPhone

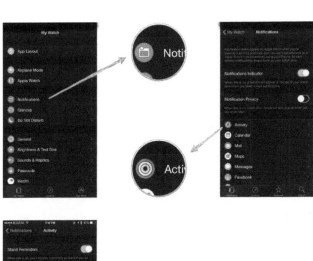

14

> ➢ On the My watch tab, select notifications
> ➢ Then tap on activity.

On the activity screen, you will find a list of apps installed on your Apple watch. You can then choose what activity or app you want to get notifications. You can switch the activity alert on or off for special challenges, goal completions, daily coaching, stand reminders or other exercise schedules towards a better health. The reminder alerts you to your prescheduled activities in case you get caught up with other tasks. The stand reminder reminds you to stand up for a few minutes especially if you have been sitted for too long.

On the top of the screen, there is a list of local apps for on your iPhone that you can customize in the Apple watch. Some of the customizable apps include messaging, mail, weather, activity, calendar, clock, phone and some others.

**To customize activity notifications,**

- o Start the Apple watch app on your phone,
- o Tap on notifications then select the apps you want.

**For instance, to customize the breathe notification,**

- o Start the watch app on your phone
- o Click on notification
- o Select breathe
- o Browse through the notification settings available for the breathe app and select your most preferred setting. You can change the number of alerts you receive each day or totally mute the notifications on days you don't want to be disturbed.

**To customize the calendar notification,**

- o Start the Apple watch app on your phone
- o Select notification
- o Tap on calendar
- o Tap on custom

o Select an upcoming event you want to be reminded of, invitations, or even toggle the calendar alert on or off.

## Customizing the mail notification

Mails are important part of our life as they contain information on our businesses, personal life, applications, projects and lots more. You wouldn't want to miss any important message in your mail because you got so busy. You can get notified as new messages drop into your mailbox by customizing your mail notification.

## To customize your mail notification

➤ Launch the watch app on your phone
➤ Click on notification
➤ Click on mail
➤ Select custom
➤ Click on "allow notifications"

You can switch the mail alerts on and off and chose your preferred alert mode for every mail account you own to easily differentiate between your messages.

## Customizing the message notification

You get different messages from people daily and sometimes, you can't seem to keep up with replying them all as you can't differentiate between the urgent, important or random messages. Customizing your message notification helps you set a priority level to each message as you receive them.

## To customize your message notification

- ➤ Start the watch app on your iPhone
- ➤ Select notifications
- ➤ Select messages
- ➤ Tap on custom

You can choose to put your message alerts on or off or select your preferred message tone and feedback. You can also choose to repeat alerts depending on the priority of the message received. This can be done by selecting important contacts or marking some contacts based on their priority level.

**How to create custom message replies on your Apple watch**

Some messages require immediate attention and responses to acknowledge that you received them, while others may only need a quick response. You can send a quick reply by using a message response. Message responses are direct and easy to send when you need them. Once you have customized your message notification to know what message was received and the urgency of its response, you need to create the perfect responses for them.

For instance, a quick message from work that requires immediate attention should not take you more than some seconds to reply. Your Apple watch may have its default message responses, but you can add your preferred texts. How does this work?

Open the watch app on your iPhone

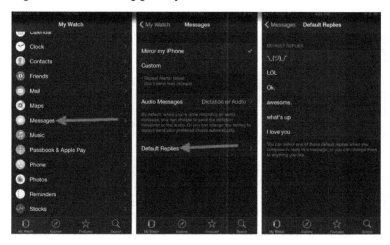

- o Select messages
- o Click on default replies
- o Click on add reply and insert your preferred responses or select a default reply to change to your preferred response.

**To delete or change custom replies on your Apple watch**

- o Open the Apple watch app on your phone
- o Select messages
- o Choose default replies
- o Select edit
- o Tap the minus sign in the red circle next to the message you want to delete
- o Choose delete

**To prioritize or rearrange your message responses**

- o Open watch app on your phone
- o Click messages
- o Click default replies
- o Tap edit
- o Click and hold the lines on the message you'd like to rearrange and drag to its intended position.

**Customizing the phone notification**

> ➤ Launch the Apple watch app on your phone
> ➤ Tap notifications
> ➤ Select phone
> ➤ Tap on custom
> ➤ Set your phone alert based on your preference.

**What to do when custom notification is not responding.**

If your custom notification is not working, you can try the following steps;

i. Deactivate and reactivate notifications. This is usually the first response to such case and usually the fastest and quickest means of resolving the issue.

ii. Delete and re-install the watch app causing the issue

iii.    Or as a last option, you can reset your Apple watch

# Customization with Apple Watch Faces

Your Apple watch is loaded with a variety of watch faces to select from. You can choose to customize these watch faces to your preference. How do you do this? It only requires a few steps to follow and voila! You begin to change from the chronograph to the Mickey Mouse watch face in just one swipe.

The watch faces available by default include

- Breathe
- Astronomy
- Activity digital
- Activity analog
- Chronograph
- Infograph
- Color
- Fire and water
- Explorer

- Kaleidoscope
- Mickey and Minnie Mouse, and so many more.

Each of these watch faces have a different capacity, density and character which determines their complication and customization. The watch face you use depends basically on your choice and preference.

The breathe watch face for instance monitors your breath and reminds you to take conscious and relaxing breaths. Its style is the only customizable feature and can be switched between Classic, Calm and Focus.

On the Breathe watch face are the following complications: Alarm, Breathe styles, Heart Rate, Mail, Reminders, Timer, Weather, Walkie-Talkie, Stopwatch, World Clock, Sunrise/Sunset, Maps, Date, Battery, Activity, Music, Messages, News and Workout.

The Chronograph watch face is like a traditional analog stopwatch that measures time as it increases. Its color and timescale is the only customizable feature on this face.

**Changing watch faces on Apple watch**

Changing the watch face on your Apple watch is simple. With a swipe, you can switch between chronograph to infograph, breathe to color, Mickey and Minnie mouse to simple and many more. It requires a little practice and then you become a watch face pro, changing your watch face like meals. To change the watch face,

> ➢ Press down the digital crown of your Apple watch to select the watch face.
> ➢ Swipe from left to right to view the available watch faces on your watch before making your choice. You may need to start from edge of your watch screen to switch faces.
> ➢ Select your most preferred watch face.

## Adding Apple watch face to your list

You can add as many styles of watch faces as you want on your list to select from. To do this,

> ➢ Open the Apple watch app on your iPhone

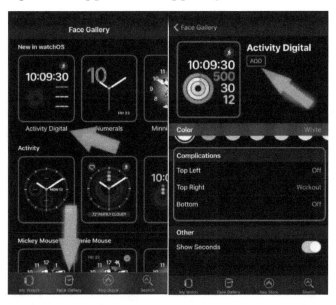

> ➢ Click on the face gallery app
> ➢ The watch faces are organized by type
> ➢ Click a watch face type from the list and select
> ➢ Tap "Add"
> ➢ Click on a watch face and then click on add.

Your watch display will automatically change to the newly selected watch face.

**Organizing the list of Apple watch faces**

You may want to keep your watch faces neatly arranged and in order for ease of selection. You may want some styles beside each other, or want to arrange based on color. However way you want it, it takes only a few simple steps.

- ➢ Open the watch app on your iPhone
- ➢ Select "My watch" tab
- ➢ Under "my faces", click edit
- ➢ On the right side of the watch face, you'll find three lines that represents the organize icon, press and hold it down
- ➢ Drag your selected watch face to the new position you want it on your list

A new order of watch faces will appear on your Apple watch.

**Setting a photo as the Apple watch face**

To set your photo as an Apple watch face, you either select one picture at a time, or add an album that gives a different picture each time you wake your watch.

To set your photo,

- ➤ Sync a photo album to your Apple watch. On your iPhone, you can create a new album and name it Apple watch photos for easy access. Then add your preferred photos to the album.
- ➤ Open the Apple watch app on your iPhone and select "My watch"
- ➤ Scroll down and choose the photo apps
- ➤ Click synced album and select your newly created album (My Apple watch photos)

The selected photos will automatically sync with your Apple watch and will be available for use at anytime with or without your iPhone. For more recent photos, you can sync your Apple watch with your iPhone's camera roll. The pictures will be added as you take new ones. With the watch face set, press and hold the screen until the customize icon comes up. Swipe to the left for photo album and select.

Select the photo watch face you prefer and click customize. This will allow you to adjust the size, color and/or position of your choice photo. To zoom your photos or view all, rotate the digital crown and select the photo you wish to add to your watch face. Once you are done, you then press in the digital crown.

When using a photo watch face, it will only display the time and date as you cannot customize complications using a personal photo watch face. You can save up to 500 personal photos on your Apple watch.

## How to delete an Apple watch face

You may get so excited by the ease of changing your watch faces and end up filling the space with more pictures than it can take. Well, it's no big deal because you can delete excess watch faces as easily as you can add them.

> ➢ Start the watch face or double press the digital crown
> ➢ Press and hold the watch face until the watch face switch comes up
> ➢ Swipe left or right to select the watch face you wish to delete
> ➢ Scroll up on the watch face
> ➢ Then click delete
> ➢ Repeat the process for all the watch faces you wish to remove.

You can also do this on your iPhone

- Open the watch app on your iPhone

- Click on 'my watch'
- Under "my faces, click edit
- Tap the minus sign next to the watch faces you wish to delete
- Then click remove

You can re-add any watch face you remove later.

## Track Health and Fitness

One of the main reasons people get the Apple Watch is to use the health and fitness tracker.

### How to set up Activity on your Apple Watch

- Go to Activity app on your iPhone.
- Click on Set up Activity.
- Type in your personal information.
- Tap Continue.
- Set your Daily Move Goal.
- Click on Set Move Goal.

## Phone Calls on the Apple Watch

Thanks to your Apple Watch, you can make or answer a call without taking your phone out of your pocket.

### Answering Phone Calls with the Apple watch

When you get a call that comes in your Apple Watch, you can either accept the call, reject the call or scroll down to send a message or answer on your iPhone.

- Click on the green phone button to answer

- Click the mute button if you need to mute a call.

- Turn the Digital Crown to either increase or reduce the volume of the call.

- Click on the red disconnect button when you are done with your call.

## Apple Watch New Features

A cool new feature on the Apple watch 5 is the detection of a hard fall when you are using the Apple Watch. When this happens, the watch will automatically vibrate on your wrist, sound an alarm, and display an alert. From there, you can decide whether to contact emergency services from the watch or dismiss the warnings.

## How to turn Fall Detection on

Fall detection feature on your Apple Watch Series 5 is off by default unless, but if you are age 65 or older, the feature automatically turns on. To manually enable the Fall Detection feature on from your iPhone:

- Go to the Watch app on your iPhone.
- Click on the 'My Watch tab' at the bottom left.

- Click on 'Emergency SOS'.

- Scroll down and turn on Fall Detection by enabling the toggle.

## How to Enable Wrist Detection

Wrist detection on for your Apple Watch must be enabled to automatically call emergency services. To enable this feature:

- Go to settings on your Apple Watch.

- Click on Passcode.

- Scroll down and enable the toggle to turn on Wrist Detection.

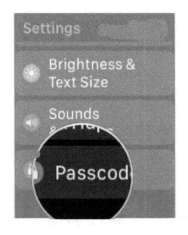 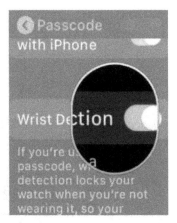

### How to make an emergency call after a fall

When you fall, you will get an alert on your Apple Watch, showing a slider for Emergency SOS and a button for I'm okay.

- To call emergency services on your Apple watch, just move the SOS slider from left to right. If you're not hurt, click on 'I fell, but I'm OK'.

- Follow the instructions from the emergency service operator.

- Tap the phone icon once you're done with your call.

- Click Yes to confirm.

**How to add friends and family to your emergency contact list**

To add emergency contacts:

- Go to the Apple Health app on your iPhone.

- Click on your Profile in the top right corner.

- Click on Medical ID.

- Click on Edit in the top right corner.

- Scroll down to the Emergency Contacts section and click on add emergency contact, which will bring up your list of contacts on your iPhone.
- Click on the contact you would like to add to your emergency contacts list.
- Click on the phone number for the contact you would like to use.
- The next step is to identify your relationship with this person.

**Noise App**

This feature when enabled, actually allows you to measure sound in your area, that is how loud the noise is so that you can protect your ears by staying away from loud noises that can damage your hearing. To enable it:

- Go to the noise app
- Scroll down and tap on enable

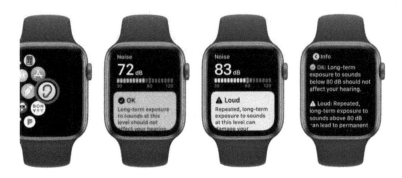

## How to customize noise alerts

- Go to Watch app on your iPhone

- Swipe down and click on Noise

- Click on "Noise Threshold" to customize alerts or disable them

- You can click the toggle next to "Environmental Sound Measurements" settings page for the Noise app if you want to disable the feature

## Hide Sensitive Information on the Watch Face

- Go to watch app on your iPhone

- Tap on Brightness and text size

- Tap on Always On

- Enable the Hide Sensitive Complications toggle

## Making Proficient Use of The Digital Crown

The digital crown on your Apple watch is quite similar to the crown on mechanical watches. Though the crown on a mechanical watch is used to set the time or date or to wind the main spring; it is not so with the Apple watch. The digital crown on an Apple watch serves the same purpose as the home button on your iPhone- you press the digital crown to return to the home screen of your Apple watch. But that's not all it serves, as you can rotate the digital crown to zoom or scroll depending on what you are doing on your Apple watch. By spinning, scrolling or pressing the digital crown, you can activate and walk through some of the many features on your Apple watch.

In short, the digital crown is an interactive tool between the watch and its apps or features and controls the borders of the watch by providing instant responses as you use the watch. The digital crown also provides a haptic feedback as you swipe or scroll through the Apple watch. With the digital crown on your Apple watch, you can do any one of the following conveniently:

**Wake up your watch**

Sometimes you may be pressed to check the time without having to lift your wrist. Gently press the digital crown to wake up your watch's display. On the other hand, you can slowly scroll up the crown to brighten the watch display. This is usually necessary if you are in a dark room and you need to check the time subtly especially when in a meeting or gathering that is taking longer time.

**Home button**

The digital crown serves as the home button for your Apple watch. Whether you are on the watch face and need to go back to the apps menu, the digital crown does the job, and if you are on the apps menu and need to go back to the clock face.

## App switch

The digital crown is a fast app switching tool. It takes you from the watch face to the most recent app on your Apple watch. The same goes for using different apps at a time, you can switch in between apps. You can leave an app and quickly load up another app, and with a double tap on the digital crown, you easily flip between apps.

## Zooming

Turning the crown front and back enables the screen to zoom in and zoom out efficiently thus providing a clearer view of apps on the small watch. You can also load certain apps on your Apple watch with the zooming effect without touching the screen though you may have to use the touchscreen to navigate the apps. The zooming effect also applies to your photos, if you have them synced to you Apple watch and if your apps are arranged in the grid view, the digital crown can help you scroll up or down the grid to select an app.

**Restarting your watch**

One other important function of the digital crown is restarting your Apple watch anytime you have issues with it and restarting seems the best option. Simply hold down the power button and the crown for a few seconds, your watch will fully restart and close down any running apps whilst the OS restarts. You won't lose any data when you do this.

**Scroll vertical Screens**

In some Apple watches, the apps are arranged vertically on the watch screen. The digital crown helps you scroll up and down the screen effectively, and in cases the digital crown moves some contents in the horizontal direction.

## Volume control

Whenever you are listening to music on your watch or iPhone, you may need to adjust the volume at some point. Scrolling the digital crown up or down helps you raise or lower your music volume or whatever you may be listening to.

## Siri

When you press down the digital crown of your Apple watch, you enable Siri that is your watch's digital voice-driven assistant. This is much easier than the conventional way of lifting your wrist to call it up.

## Take a screenshot

To take a screenshot on your Apple watch, you press down the digital crown with the side button. This is possible only after you have enabled screenshot on your iPhone. To enable screenshot, launch the watch app on your phone; go to 'my watch', tap general and switch enable screenshots to on.

## Quit an app

Sometimes an app may cause a nuisance on your watch by being unresponsive, and you may only have to force quit or restart your Apple watch. To forcefully quit the unresponsive app, press down the side button until you see the power screen and press down the digital crown until it returns to the watch face.

To force restart, press and hold down the side button and digital crown until your watch screen goes dark and the Apple logo reappears.

## Turn off display

In order to save your watch's battery power, you may sometimes need to increase or lower the screen brightness. To adjust the brightness, turn the crown up or down depending on the result you want.

## Time setting

This may seem unnecessary because the time on your Apple watch works with the set time on the iPhone it is connected to, but you may sometimes need to set your time ahead of the normal time in order to keep up with a schedule, plan or workout.

**Using digital touch to send sketches, heartbeat and taps on the Apple watch**

The digital touch feature on your Apple watch is used to send heartbeat, taps or sketches to share with a friend. It is easier if you both have an Apple watch because the digital touch messages can be felt on the wrist.

- To send a digital touch, select message, click on the drawing canvas to open. Sketch an image of your choice on the screen. Tap the dot icon to change color. Stop drawing to send.
- To send a tap, tap the screen as many times as you want, click the dot to change color, stop tapping to send.
- To send a kiss, tap your two fingers on the screen one or more times. The kisses will be

shown on your watch screen. Stop tapping to send.

- To share your heartbeat, place two fingers on your watch screen until your heart shows on the screen and you feel your heartbeat. Lift your fingers to send.

- To see a digital touch message from your friend, tap the notification on your Apple watch.

# Amazing Apple Watch Tips and Tricks

Are you the type that uses your device only for the stuffs you know? That can be boring, you know. And you can't purchase a device like the Apple watch just to check the time or send messages. Definitely not! Your Apple watch has more functions on it than you may know about, but don't worry, we'll show you a few tips and tricks you wouldn't believe your watch is capable of.

## Get Apple Watch to tell time

One of the coolest things of the apple watch is for it to tell you the time. To do this, just place two fingers on the screen on the apple watch.

## Locate your iPhone

With your Apple watch, you can easily find your misplaced or hidden iPhone by tracking it with your watch. Truth is we've all been there at one point. So, this tip works for us all.

From your watch face, scroll up to start the control center where you tap a blue button that reads "ping iPhone". Your iPhone will give a loud noise wherever it is and there, you have your phone. In some cases, you may need more than the ring to find your phone, you can as well activate the LED flash on your camera to make your phone more obvious to find.

**Mute alerts**

There are days you crave for me-time, or probably stuck in a meeting that needs your full concentration, but then you forgot to mute your watch. To mute the alerts without causing much distraction, you only need to place your palm over the display for about three seconds to mute any sound. To activate this, open the Apple watch app on your iPhone then select "my watch", sounds and haptic and cover to mute.

## Enlarge on-screen text

Being a small device, you may need to opt for bigger texts sometimes which can be done easily on your watch. To enlarge the texts, select settings, then brightness and text size. Choose your preferred text size.

## Take a screenshot

One would think such a small device cannot take a screenshot, but the Apple watch can. You may need to save your digital touch messages or sketches or keep record of your daily activity achievement. Take a screenshot of this by pressing down the side button and digital crown at the same time.

## Force restart

Just like a phone, you can forcefully restart your Apple watch whenever it is not responding or misbehaving. You do this by pressing both the side button and the digital crown for some seconds (10 seconds at most) or until you see the Apple logo.

**Pre-compose messages**

Though the Apple watch is not big enough for typing, but you can sync some pre-composed messages on your iPhone with the Apple watch. This is usually necessary when you can't answer a call or a message needs an immediate response from you. You can tap on any of these pre-composed messages to auto send. To add your pre-composed messages, open my watch app on your iPhone and go to messages, to default replies. Tap edit and put in the message of your choice.

**Call holding**

In cases where your iPhone is nowhere close, you can answer a call on your Apple watch and place it on hold until you can find your iPhone. The caller will be notified by a short beeping sound which stops immediately you can answer with your phone.

**Add and play music**

There is enough storage space on your Apple watch to save your songs and playlist when you don't want to use your iPhone. This feature is perfect for work out, early morning exercise and moments of meditation. If you are a music lover this tip is for you. Simply connect to your wireless headset or ear buds and you are good to go.

The easiest way is to sync the playlist on your iPhone with your Apple watch and wait till the sync is complete. It is advisable to do this while your Apple watch is charging and be sure to keep both devices connected.

To play your music, press the digital crown on your watch to open your apps and click on the music icon where you find the synced playlists.

**Unlock your Mac**

The Apple's ability to sync between its devices is one great feature you can't ignore. If you are an Apple brand lover, it is easy to use your Apple watch to unlock your Mac without a need for password; you only need to make sure both devices are signed into the same iCloud account. You are one of the few who knows about this tip, and we hope it comes in handy.

**Take photos**

Yes, you can actually take photos with your Apple watch. But that's not possible; no Apple watch model comes with camera. Well, that's true but Apple has pre-installed camera app on Apple watch that allows you to use your watch as a shutter trigger for your iPhone camera. This feature comes in handy for group pictures you would like to be included in.

**Use Siri on your Apple watch**

Now that your voice-driven assistant has been improved on, you no longer need to activate operations on your watch by saying Hey, Siri. Sometimes it feels awkward especially when you are in crowded places, but you don't need to go through that anymore. You only need to enable the wrist raise option to automatically start up the assistant. In other cases, you may just need to hold down the pipe to start the assistant.

**Use pictures as watch faces**

This has been discussed earlier under settings. Your Apple watch doesn't have to be a boring device because you can personalize it with different pictures from your device.

**Monitor data usage**

The Apple watch consumes less data, but can also help you watch your data usage so you don't go over your monthly plan. To activate this, open the app on your watch and check the cellular menu option to view your data usage. You can also identify the app that consumes most data so as to lower the frequency of use.

**Water eject feature**

The Apple watch has had a waterproof feature since Series 2. It is amazing that you can go to swim without removing your wristwatch. This means you can record how many laps you did while swimming, without having to bother about watch damage. The Apple watch has an eject mode that allows you to free every water drop left inside your watch.

The water eject feature functions automatically, but you can also operate it manually by taking a swipe up the watch screen to the Apple watch control center. There you'll find a water droplet sign, press and follow the instruction to twist the digital crown to eject. You can as well tap the droplet sign before going into the pool.

**Enable the Mickey and Minnie feature**
We all have our down times when we need a little fun to make us lively. The Mickey and Minnie feature can serve as your mood lifter during those periods. By tapping on the Mickey and Minnie watch face, they tell you the time in their funny voices. There, that got you, but make sure you have it activated by enabling the "Tap to speak" feature under settings.

## Clear notifications

Sometimes, there are so many notifications piled up on the notification bar and it feels tasking to read through. You can clear these notifications on your watch without opening your phone. At some points though, you may want to keep some important notifications you need to attend to later. For instance, a message from a friend you don't wish to ignore, and clearing all notifications may also mean clearing the message notification, which you don't want to miss. Here is the way around it, you can simply press down the digital crown to go back to the home screen or whatever you were doing on the device without tampering with the notifications until you are ready to sort them out.

## Mark mail messages

Your Apple watch has no keypad to type messages or reply chats, but you can actually star important messages you want to reply for easy identification.

Hold down the message(s) you wish to mark and tap flag.

## Monitor activities

With your apple watch as a new companion, you don't need to skip any workout session in order to stay trim, fit and in shape. Your watch will help you monitor your daily exercises and remind you of the need to close the gaps if there's any. The apple watch series 4 also enables you to check your ECG by pressing down on the digital crown for about 30 seconds once the ECG app is enabled. And lastly, you can use the Breathe app to relax and concentrate especially after a very long and stressful day. Open the breathe app, then use the digital crown to set the minutes and number of breathes you'd like to track, then click on start.

## Final Note

Thank you for purchasing this book. Now that you have this guide, I am sure that using your Apple watch will no longer be as complicated as you thought it would. We'd love to hear from you even as we trust you to enjoy and get the best of all features in your Apple watch.

www.ingramcontent.com/pod-product-compliance
Lightning Source LLC
Chambersburg PA
CBHW070855070326
40690CB00009B/1851